James C. Santana de Oliveira

Green IT

James C. Santana de Oliveira

Green IT

Essential tool for environmental damage caused by IT

ScienciaScripts

Imprint
Any brand names and product names mentioned in this book are subject to trademark, brand or patent protection and are trademarks or registered trademarks of their respective holders. The use of brand names, product names, common names, trade names, product descriptions etc. even without a particular marking in this work is in no way to be construed to mean that such names may be regarded as unrestricted in respect of trademark and brand protection legislation and could thus be used by anyone.

Cover image: www.ingimage.com

This book is a translation from the original published under ISBN 978-3-330-99834-6.

Publisher:
Sciencia Scripts
is a trademark of
Dodo Books Indian Ocean Ltd. and OmniScriptum S.R.L publishing group

120 High Road, East Finchley, London, N2 9ED, United Kingdom
Str. Armeneasca 28/1, office 1, Chisinau MD-2012, Republic of Moldova, Europe
Managing Directors: Ieva Konstantinova, Victoria Ursu
info@omniscriptum.com

Printed at: see last page
ISBN: 978-620-8-64444-4

I dedicate this work to everyone who has supported me and given me strength up to this point.

ACKNOWLEDGEMENTS

To my supervisor Prof. Esp. José Márcio Mathias and my co-supervisor Prof. Me. Maria do Carmo Vara Lopes Orsi, who helped me at every stage of this work.

To Professors Walter Masson and Osvaldo D'Estefano Rosica, members of the examining board and responsible for assessing the TG.

To Professor Neucy Donizeti Xavier Pinto from the PTG course and Professor Patrícia Gláucia Moreno from the TG course, for their tips and patience.

To Professor Eoná Moro Ribeiro for correcting and approving the abstract of this work in the Book of Abstracts of the XI Fatec Tatuí Technology Symposium - Participatory Management of Water Resources (2016).

To Professors Dr Gustavo k. Montanha and Me. Marcelo S. Denadai for approving the expanded abstract of this work at the 5th Scientific and Technological Conference of Fatec Botucatu (2016), available in the electronic annals of Jornacitec ISSN: 2318-535X.

"Despite the growing tendency of technology companies and service providers to use the term sustainable, the industry is far from operating in a sustainable environment. "

SIMON MINGAY, 2007.

SUMMARY

The aim of this paper is to present Green IT as an essential tool for controlling pollution and environmental damage caused by the IT sector, given that the excessive increase in hardware consumption in the IT sector has constantly damaged the environment. The high cost of electricity and the continuous replacement of IT materials is one of the main problems for nature, as it contaminates the soil through the improper disposal of highly toxic components. In Brazil, there is still no standard or law that regulates all IT processes, including their interaction with the environment. This bibliographical research will look at the concept of Green IT based on the article by the Gartner Institute, called Green IT: a new industry shock wave by Simon Mingay (2007), which will analyse its three factors: its policies and legislation, information and organisational strategies and ReDesign, ReUse, ReCycle, comprising its main certifications and seals. Finally, the European Union's legislation REACH - Registration, Evaluation and Authorisation of Chemicals, the European Parliament's RoHS directive and the European Commission's Cap and Trade environmental policy make Green IT possible. Its proposal is to give differentiated treatment to each stage of the useful life of IT equipment, defining specific actions that affect the way equipment and products are developed, how purchasing strategies are defined by companies, how technology is used and also the processes of disposal, reuse and recycling.

Keywords: Green IT, Sustainability, Legislation.

SUMMARY

CHAPTER 1

INTRODUCTION

One of IT's biggest problems is its increasing integration with the environment. This increase is due to investment in technology by companies in all sectors, with the aim of producing more, in less time and at a lower cost. However, the materials used in this sector are replaced all the time, such as monitors, notebooks and their implements, which end up in a landfill or disposed of irregularly.

In Brazil there is still no standard or law that regulates all IT processes, including the environment. Law No. 12.305 of 2 August 2010 in Article 33 (BRASIL, 2010), with emphasis on paragraph VI - electrical and electronic products and their components, indirectly mentions the implementation of reverse logistics systems, through the return of products after use by the consumer.

This sector requires more sustainable practices and this demand has led to the emergence of the Green IT methodology, where the main objective is to apply sustainable techniques to all processes, aiming at organisational practices to reduce environmental pollution, reuse parts and equipment, and reduce costs with electricity consumption (MINGAY, 2007).

This paper will look at the concept of Green IT based on the Gartner Institute article Green IT: a new industry shock wave by Simon Mingay (2007), which will also analyse the three factors of Green IT: policies and legislation, information and organisational strategies and ReDesign, ReUse, ReCycle.

Understanding the European Union legislation (2006) REACH-Registration, Evaluation and Authorisation of Chemicals, the European

Parliament's RoHS directive (2011) and the Cap and Trade environmental policy according to the European Commission (2016) that make Green IT possible.

1.1 BACKGROUND

Green IT is still little discussed and applied to organisational strategy in Brazil. The study's creator was Simon Mingay in his article Green IT: a new industry shock wave (MINGAY, 2007), in which the term is presented for the first time and defined conceptually. It brings up new practices and solutions for the IT area, as an essential tool for controlling pollution and environmental damage caused by the sector.

1.2 OBJECTIVES

1.2.1 General objective

Presenting Green IT as an essential tool for controlling pollution and environmental damage caused by the usual completeness of the IT area.

1.2.2 Specific objectives

- Explain the technological evolution of IT as a whole;
- Address the concept of Green *IT* through research into articles published on the subject;
- Conceptualise the three factors of Green *IT* that guide its entire structure and implementation:
- Identify the REACH legislation, the RoHS directive and the Cap and Trade environmental policy and their correlations with Green IT;

CHAPTER 2

THEORETICAL BACKGROUND

It goes from the origins of Green IT based on social and business issues, to the benefits it brings to organisations and, in this context, how the adoption of this tool contributes to the environment and generates improvements for companies.

2.1 BUSINESS TECHNOLOGY DEVELOPMENTS

The introduction of technology into the business world began around the 1950s, when a procedure was automated and checked. Information was considered a necessary bureaucratic requirement that reduced the cost of issuing lots of paperwork (SACILOTTI, 2011, p.24). The following figure shows this insertion.

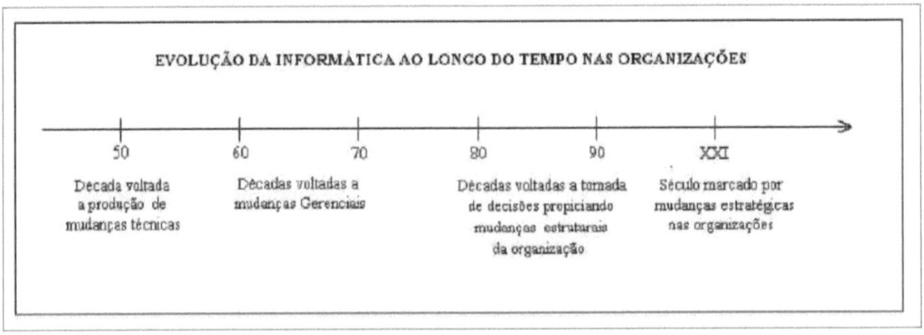

Figure 1: Evolution of IT over time in organisations

SOURCE: SACILOTTI (2011, p.24).

Sacilotti (2011, p.24) states that in the 1960s, systems brought about managerial and behavioural changes, and also began to influence people's actions. In this decade, information was seen as a support for the company's general purposes, helping to manage various activities. This early period became known as the Data Processing Era, whose main objective was to automate operational functions on a large scale (FRESCHI, 2013, p.3).

In the 1970s, costs were reduced and processing speed increased, computers began to issue management reports, where data began to be used as a source of information. Freschi (2013, p.2) defines this moment as the Age of Information Systems,

In the 1980s, information began to be understood as a factor in the control and management of the entire organisation, which helped and accelerated decision-making processes. With the creation of microcomputers, there was a change of concept in business computing. Data, which had previously been centralised on mainframes, began to be placed on the desks of users and managers (FRESCHI, 2013, p.3).

From the 1990s onwards, information began to be recognised as a strategic resource, a source of competitive advantage to guarantee a company's survival, and IT then began to expand across the board. Freschi (2013, p.3) emphasises that this ushered in the Information Technology Age, focused on the strategic importance of IT incorporated into companies, reinforcing this trend with the arrival of the internet, giving rise to e-business.

Technology was not as widespread as it is today, and the role of IT was simply to build increasingly robust hardware and software to process large amounts of data. According to Laurindo (2001, p.161) IT has evolved from a traditional administrative support orientation to a strategic role within the organisation, more specifically as shown in the figure below.

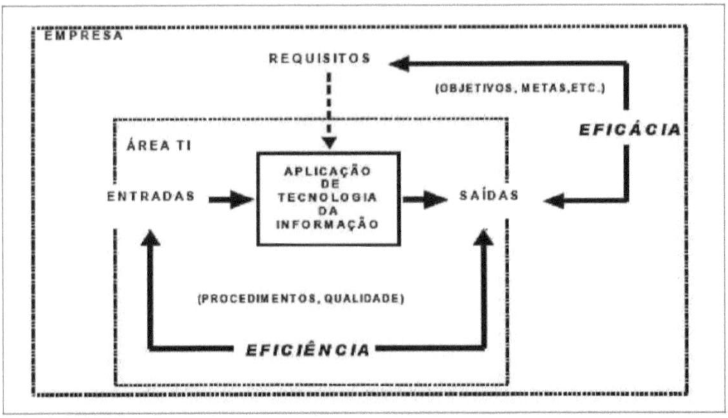

Figure 2: Efficiency and effectiveness of an information system

SOURCE: Adapted from MAGGIOLINI, 1981 apud LAURINDO (2001, p.162).

Figure 2 shows that the evolution of technology has turned IT into a strategic tool for a company, where all the inputs, processes and outputs are managed. This management is necessary to measure efficiency in processes and effectiveness in defining organisational objectives.

IT has moved on from focusing on accessing data and information to creating applications, accessing the web and then business processes, ceasing to be just a support and becoming an area of paramount importance to the organisation.

If companies don't adapt to new hardware technologies, their computer procedures become unviable, as they become obsolete from time to time and need to be replaced and disposed of, generating an excess of consumption and, consequently, a large production of electronic waste, depleting natural resources and thus affecting the environment and people.

2.1.1 Electronic waste and society

Electronic waste is defined as all the waste resulting from the rapid obsolescence of electro-electronic equipment, including devices made up almost entirely of electronic circuits such as televisions, mobile phones and computers (FAVERA, 2008, p.1).

Table 1 shows the main toxic components of an electronic product and their effects on humans.

Table 1: Components and their effects on human health

Component	Health Effects	Where it is used
Lead	Causes damage to the nervous and blood systems	Computer, mobile phone, television
Mercury	Causes brain and liver damage	Computer, monitor and flat screen TV
Cadmium	Causes poisoning, damage to bones, kidneys, lungs and affects the nervous system	Computer, old tube monitors, lap top batteries
Arsenic	Causes skin diseases, damages the nervous system and can cause lung cancer	Mobile phone
Beryllium	Causes lung cancer	Computer, mobile phone
Flame retardants (BRT)	Cause hormonal, nervous and reproductive disorders	Various components electronic devices to prevent fires
PVC	If burnt and inhaled, it can cause respiratory problems	In wires, to insulate current

SOURCE: FAVERA (2008, p.4).

Electronic waste, including computer equipment, disposed of incorrectly in the environment harms the soil with chemical substances that seep into it and, when they come into contact with the groundwater, contaminate plants and animals through the water. These substances include mercury, cadmium, arsenic, copper, lead and aluminium. (FAVERA, 2008, p.5).

What also leads society to discard is the acquisition of new hardware, because they have lost the habit of using it until the end of its useful life, and this is constant consumerism. According to Favera (2008, p.3), the components of this waste also contain highly dangerous substances that can harm people and the environment. Among the most toxic constituents are low boiling point metals, which when burnt and inhaled by people produce effects on the blood, neurological and respiratory systems.

Table 1 shows how each stage in the life cycle of a piece of technological equipment affects the environment.

Table 1: Overview of raw materials, production process, use, reuse, recycling and disposal of IT equipment

Product	Raw materials	Production Process	Utilisation	Reuse / Recycling / Disposal
Computer equipment	Plastic, metals, solvents, adhesives, etc. Environmental impacts: use of non-renewable natural resources (oil in the form of plastic and precious heavy metals). Emissions of volatile organic compounds (VOC), ammonia, hexafluoride sulfur, which contribute to global warming.	Heavy and precious metals are used in the manufacture of electronic chips; these can be toxic to humans, animals and persistent in the environment. The use of solvents and toxic substances contributes to toxic atmospheric emissions (VOCs, dorofluorocarbons (CFCs), ozone-depleting substances (ODS)), as well as producing toxic effluents and waste with organic solvents, heavy metals, among others.	Monitors (cathode ray tubes -CRT or liquid crystal *display* - LCD) produce non-ionising electromagnetic radiation; there are publications reporting health and safety risks in the use of this equipment.	Packaging and paper are overused; plastics are not biodegradable. Various components are dangerous for the environment, such as: electrical components (heavy metals), cathode ray tubes (lead, arsenic, mercury, cadmium, boron, flame retardants and polychlorinated biphenyl - PCB). Inadequate disposal can therefore contaminate groundwater, surface water and soil.

SOURCE: BRESCANSIN (2015, p.39)

Most of the time, people contaminate themselves with this waste when they directly handle electronic boards and their components in open dumps. Favera (2008, p.5) states that this happens all the time in African countries, where rubbish is incinerated after checking the materials it contains. This process of burning halogenated chlorides and bromides, which are used in plastics, generates highly toxic dioxides and furans, which are carried by the wind to areas close to the dump.

Electronic waste has caused social damage, and Favera (2008, p.5) cites the main factors as being the lack of laws that make manufacturers responsible for correct disposal, the lack of supervision regarding the destination of materials for recycling and the ineffectiveness of consumer information on the correct way to dispose of electronic products.

Globally, Favera (2008, p.6) reported on an investigation by Greenpeace, which identified highly toxic electronic waste dumps in Ghana, with containers bearing false seals from Germany, Korea, Switzerland and the Netherlands. The workers at the site destroy computers and televisions with stones in search of valuable metals, and then burn the plastic, casings and cables.

2.1.2 The relationship between business and the environment

According to Silva (2013, p.334 and 335), the strengthening of the environmental debate has led to increased political, social and economic pressure on business sectors to change the way they relate to the environment, demonstrating a greater socio-environmental commitment through environmental management and control measures with an emphasis on preventative strategies.

Brazil's environmental policy has been highlighted, with advanced legal frameworks, but it is worth remembering that according to Silva (2013, p. 335) there is no point in having a great policy if it is not complied with. The ultimate goal of companies should not be restricted to complying with legal regulations, but this should be the initial objective if they are to be truly socially and environmentally responsible.

In Brazil, the milestone for environmental laws was the Vargas period, which according to Silva was:

> When the Forest Code, the Water Code and the Mining Code were instituted in Brazil in 1934, all with the priority objectives of managing access to and use of natural resources, in view of the processes of urbanisation and industrialisation in Brazilian society. The post-1970s period, which marks the modern environmental issue in Brazil, sees the formulation of a more elaborate body of law and, although it is still characterised by developmentalist motivations, it already has other influences deriving from the domestic and international environmental debate that was then asserting itself and expanding. (SILVA, 2013, p.339)

This period saw the emergence of governmental systems such as the Special Secretariat for the Environment (SEMA) and the Brazilian Institute for the Environment and Renewable Natural Resources (IBAMA) in 1989. The Ministry of the Environment was created in 1993, the National Water Agency - ANA in 2001 and the Chico Mendes Institute for Biodiversity Conservation - ICMBio in 2007 (SILVA, 2013, p.339).

In terms of culture, Silva (2013, p. 341) states that in the 1970s, the environment was only the focus of ecologists, with a lack of interest on the part of much of society, where environmental damage was seen as a natural process and necessary for economic and social development. In the 1980s, environmental groups began to play a more active and direct role in directing corporate environmental strategies .

The highlight of the interconnection between the environment and companies came in 1992, at the United Nations Conference on Environment and Development, RIO 92, as Silva (2013, 0.342) says that this conference represented the peak of the movement in favour of environmental sustainability, and was the initial catalyst for the strongest and most consistent criticism of the terminal state of a development model that grew up in conflict with the dynamics of nature.

Companies acquire a vision of social and environmental responsibility the moment they become aware of their role in this regard. It thus goes through stages of maturity (Tachizawa, 2010, p.67 and 68). The first stage is when the organisation takes no responsibility in society, taking no action or promoting ethical behaviour.

In the second stage, the organisation recognises the impacts caused by its processes, products and services, presenting isolated actions to try to minimise them. Thirdly, it begins to systematise processes to assess its impacts, involving social issues where it operates.

When the company starts to implement this assessment and understand the issues of interest to society, the involvement of those interested in social development increases, which is the fourth stage. Once the process is systematised, the fifth stage is reached, where social issues are anticipated and discussed, and the organisation begins to exercise its responsibilities and role in society.

Currently, the National Solid Waste Policy (PNRS) of 2010 has regulated the treatment of waste in general, although it does not specify a standard for electronic waste, it can mostly be applied to this type of material. Boechat (2015) points out that this policy establishes that every company is responsible for separating and correctly disposing of the waste they produce, including industry, commerce, municipalities and consumers

This new scenario between the environment and the company leads managers to have social and environmental responsibility, which is best defined as effectiveness, i.e. related to satisfying society, meeting social, economic and cultural requirements, based on the assumption that every organisation exists to meet social needs (TACHIZAWA , 2010, p.55).

2.2 GREEN IT

Before identifying the main concepts of Green IT, it is worth highlighting the definition of IT, which according to Filleti (2015, p.3), there are various approaches to IT, but the two main aspects are the functional view and its applicability to business and the other point of view, IT is characterised as a set of solutions and activities that enable the storage, access, transmission, production, security, use of information, operational and functional efficiency.

For Marroni (2014, p.12) green IT was born out of a need to control the impacts caused by the consumption of information technology by companies, industries and society in general. MINGAY (2007, p.1) defines Green IT, in the context of a company, as the optimised use of information and communication technologies to manage the sustainability of the company's operations and supply chain, as well as its products, services and resources throughout their life cycle.

Green IT makes it possible to balance environmental impacts through process management, generating environmentally sustainable development, i.e. the necessary economic growth while preserving the environment and social development and not depleting future resources. Mingay (2007, p.2) points out that operations within a company are often the tip of an iceberg that hides environmental impacts, which is why Green IT manages and optimises all resources, including the life cycle of IT equipment, its infrastructure and efficiency.

Mingay (2007, p.2) states that in order to implement the Green IT strategy, an environmentally sustainable policy must be structured within the company, which requires an environmental assessment.

Another definition of Green IT is presented by Moraes (2015):

> The Green IT proposal is to give differentiated treatment to each stage of the useful life of IT equipment, defining specific actions that affect the way equipment and products are developed, how purchasing strategies are defined by companies, how technology is used and also the processes of disposal, reuse and recycling. It is, therefore, the integration of various practices, from energy management, virtualisation, improvements in cooling systems, recycling, to the proper disposal of electronic products, in short the adaptation of the entire Information Technology infrastructure to adjust it to the requirements of sustainability (BRAYNER, RAMOS and BRAYNER, 2013 apud MORAES 2015, p. 711 and 712).

Green IT will not be momentary, but represents the beginning of a significant change. Unlike today's fads, there is political influence and science evaluating climate change that is leading us towards a low-carbon economy (Mingay, 2007, p3). State, national and regional governments, including the United Kingdom, the European Union, Australia, California, the G8 and others, are in the midst of deciding on measures to control the emission of carbon dioxide (CO2).

According to Mingay (2007, p.3) there will be cuts in greenhouse gas emissions of 25 per cent by 2020 and 60 to 80 per cent by 2050, making it necessary to look at how these changes might affect the IT sector and its infrastructure. The IT industry is under increasing scrutiny from non-governmental agencies such as WWF and Greenpeace, which have created reports on the impacts of IT on the environment, prompting IT managers to look for solutions before it's too late.

IT equipment and infrastructure are energy inefficient, the IT industry uses a lot of resources throughout its life cycle, with limited success in reuse and recycling. The more environmental issues associated with industries are discussed, the more legislation will be imposed, such as REACH and RoHS (MINGAY, 2007, p.5).

Lunardi (2012) provides an overview of the implementation of IT in companies and the Green

IT, differentiating one from the other:

> The adoption of Green IT differs from the adoption of any other IT, especially because of the importance that ethical and sustainability issues have in the decision-making process. While the adoption of IT is usually motivated by the potential economic benefits of using this technology, Green IT practices are also motivated by being a concern for the planet, even if the economic benefits may not be tangible in the short term (LUNARDI, 2012, p.12).

Lunardi (2012, p.10 and 11) carried out a survey and content analysis of 202 articles, categorising the main Green IT practices adopted by organisations. Overall, 37 practices were identified and grouped into seven categories.

Table 2: Main Green IT practices adopted by organisations

Green IT practices	n
Awareness-raising practices	
awareness campaigns	15
green suppliers	13
sustainability policy	13
teleworking/video conferencing	7
green building	3
sustainability committees	1
energy efficiency analysis	1
Green *Datacentre*	
server consolidation	39
desktop consolidation	15
datacentre modernisation	15
outsourcing of servers	3
Disposal and recycling	
recycling parts, cartridges and equipment	16
correct disposal	13
collecting materials	8
donation or delivery of equipment	7
encouragement for recyclers	4
regulatory laws	2
Irade-in (incentive to hand in old equipment when buying new)	2
Alternative energy sources	
use of renewable energies	9
using heat for other purposes	1
water utilisation	1
Hardware	
more efficient equipment	25
replacing CRT monitors with LCD	10
elimination of harmful components in products	6
new products with recycled components	3
extending the life cycle of products	2
Print	
print outsourcing	8
monitor impressions	7
digitising documents	6
double-sided printing	6
printer consolidation	4
use of recycled paper	2

use of multifunctional devices	1
Software	
energy management systems	9
efficient applications	7
control systems (gas emissions, water quality)	7
system to design more efficient products	1

SOURCE: LUNARDI, 2012, p.11

The first category includes practices such as internal awareness campaigns about the environmental impacts that companies cause, the search for green suppliers (those who are environmentally responsible), sustainability policies to reduce the impact of IT, videoconferencing to avoid transport costs, the construction of ecological buildings, the creation of company committees to discuss sustainability and energy efficiency analyses based on IT equipment (LUNARDI, 2012, p.12).

The green datacentre category includes the practices of consolidating desktops and servers (virtualisation), modernising datacentres and outsourcing servers. Lunardi defines server consolidation in contrast to IT thinking:

> While the common thinking in IT was to have one server per service, in order to guarantee greater security and availability of services on the network (at a high idle rate), server consolidation consists of using just one physical machine with several virtual machines, one for each server. This new approach guarantees the isolation of servers and has the advantages of increasing their utilisation rate, reducing operating costs, creating more flexible environments and reducing administration costs (LUNARDI, 2012, p.13).

With regard to the consolidation of desktops, the use of thin client terminals has been highlighted, where users are connected to a central server that carries out all the processing without any loss to the end user, while saving almost 80 per cent more energy than a normal workstation (GUPTA, 2010 apud LUNARDI 2012, p.13).

Disposal and recycling practices concern the recycling of parts, cartridges and equipment, the correct disposal of components that can be reused or that need to be discarded, the collection of materials, the donation of obsolete equipment, the encouragement given to recyclers, regulatory laws and the incentive to hand in old equipment when buying new, known as trade-in (LUNARDI 2012, p.13).

One of the most difficult practices is that of alternative energy sources, where the IT area has yet to adapt to the use of renewable energy and the use of heat in datacentres, but which does not affect water consumption so much.

In the Hardware category, the main practices are the development of more energy-efficient and economical equipment, the replacement of CRT monitors with LCDs, the elimination of harmful components in products, the use of recycled components in the manufacture of new products and increasing the life cycle of products (LUNARDI 2012, p.14).

With regard to the application of Green IT practices linked to printing, Lunardi (2012) points out that:

> The biggest concern is still the use of paper, but by taking a few steps, organisations can reduce the environmental impact of printers and printing. The practices used have been outsourcing printing, monitoring printing, digitising documents, double-sided printing, consolidating printers, using recycled paper and using multifunction printers (LUNARDI, 2012, p.15).

Software practices can be seen from the perspective of making computer programs more efficient, consuming less energy, optimising their processing and disabling functions or devices when not in use, or managing energy consumption according to the use of the equipment, controlling gas emissions or water quality and designing new, more efficient products (LUNARDI 2012, p.15).

Based on the research of Mingay (2007) and Lunardi (2012), the following is a figure that seeks to exemplify the company's Green IT implementation actions:

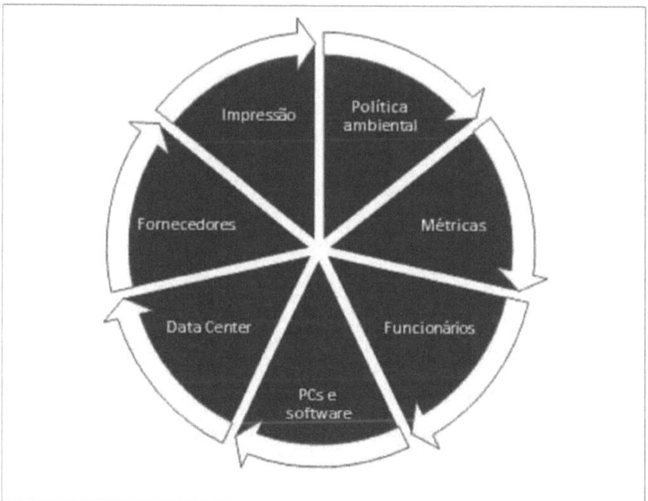

Figure 3: Cycle of practices that permeate Green IT

SOURCE: Own elaboration.

Firstly, it's worth remembering that figure 3 has arrows indicating a continuous and interconnected cycle, because each stage depends on the other for the fulfilment of the goal.

Green IT, and its evaluation must be carried out repeatedly. Initially, the environmental policy action leads the company to define strategies that reduce the environmental impact of IT, checking which processes and how they harm the environment.

Metrics make it possible to find out how the environmental policy is positively affecting the company, i.e. to discover and quantify energy efficiency, emissions of polluting gases and waste generation, so that reduction targets can be created. However, if employees don't agree with the new habits, the implementation will go backwards, which is why it's interesting to determine everyone's responsibility in this new policy.

When it comes to PCs and software, it's important to carry out power management, removing the screen saver, dimming the screen and applying sleep modes all generate significant cost savings.

Mingay (2007) emphasises cooling in his explanation of the data centre, pointing out that air flow, fans, air conditioning and distribution losses should be analysed and, if possible, corrected with changes to the infrastructure.

The penultimate action in the cycle relates to suppliers, i.e. before purchasing a product it is proposed to check its environmental performance throughout its life cycle, whether it complies with REACH legislation and the RoHS directive, and whether it is at least EPEAT certified.

When it comes to printing, the aim is to quantify the volume of prints made, whether daily, weekly or monthly. However, it is up to each employee to realise at the time of printing whether it is really necessary, if the document is to be discarded or archived later, it can be printed on both sides of the sheet (Mingay, 2007).

2.2.1 Green IT factors

The three factors governing Green IT are related to policies and legislation concerning business strategies, indicating the tactics and goals set by organisations. Information and organisational strategies, which refer to the ability of employees to build, and ReDesign, ReUse, ReCycle, which refers to environmental policies and actions developed on the basis of IT infrastructure and support.

In the concepts discussed by Ladeira (2009), Green IT has three factors:

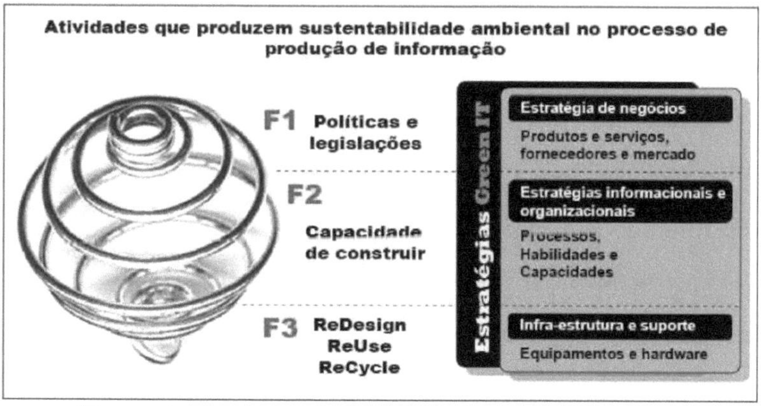

Figure 4: Framework for analysing the activities that generate Green IT

SOURCE: LADEIRA, 2009, p.9

Ladeira (2009, p.9) says that this spiral separates the three factors, but they are united because they are part of Green IT activities. The flattened disc shape with a spherical cluster of the spiral helps us understand that Green IT activities revolve around a central point, moving away from or closer to the point, depending on the direction the curve travels.

Factor F1 concerns policies and legislation relating to business strategies. It focuses directly on relationships with suppliers and the market, with a view to greater environmental/economic sustainability of products and services. This factor brings together the policies and actions that organisations use to produce environmental sustainability in the information production process (LADEIRA, 2009, p, 10), seeking to analyse and plan ways of managing electronic waste.

Factor F2 explains the employees' ability to construct information and organisational strategies. The focus of this factor is the organisation's ability to work on its capacities and skills to develop environmentally responsible processes. It measures the ability to build more environmentally friendly information and organisational policies in the information production process (LADEIRA, 2009, p, 10), with the emphasis on building a structure for sustainability to be efficient, i.e. throughout the EEE process (life cycle).

Factor F3 refers to the environmental policies and actions developed based on IT infrastructure and support. The focus of this factor was on environmental actions involving the equipment and hardware of organisations, through the concepts of ReDesign, ReUse and ReCycle, measuring the capacity of the actions of each in the information production process. (LADEIRA, 2009, p, 10 and 11).

ReDesign seeks solutions for EEE waste, increasing its useful life cycle by studying its material composition and toxicity. ReUse seeks to reuse EEE products, increasing their utilisation and components, thereby reducing waste and reducing material substitution and ReCycle aims to create recycling systems and evaluate the collection and processing of electronic products, paying attention to existing environmental policies.

2.2.2 Certifications and seals relevant to Green IT

Green IT certification for companies assesses IT sustainability through strict standards that include guidelines, procedures and monitoring specifications. An example is VILT, a global IT company specialising in the Enterprise Content Management (ECM) sector, which seeks to maximise the energy efficiency of the contracting company by purchasing certified hardware, promoting and guaranteeing the recycling and biodegradability of products and working with suppliers who are concerned about the environment.

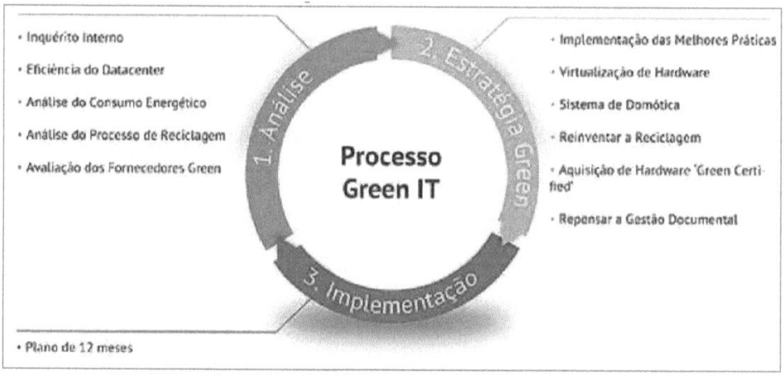

Figure 5: Green IT process

The Green IT process applied by VILT comprises three key stages: analysis (weaknesses, strengths, opportunities), definition of a Green IT Strategy and implementation of a 12-month plan.

The main areas for strategic Green IT actions defined by VILT as basic requirements for obtaining certification for a company are set out in figure 6.

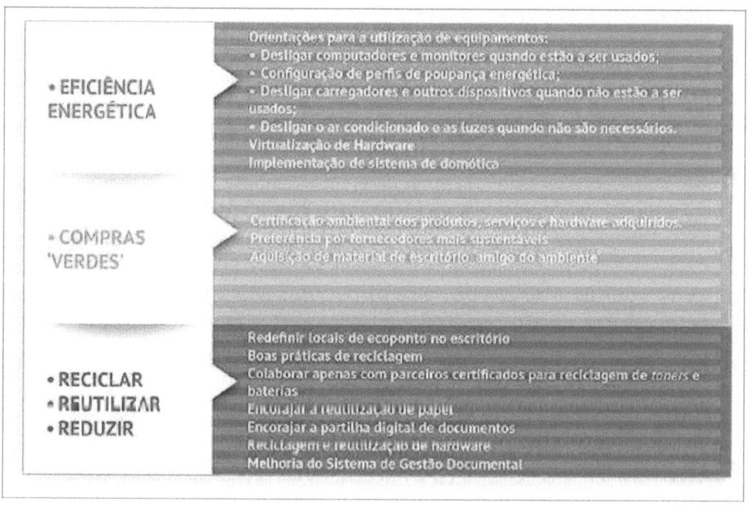

Figura 6: Our Green policy

SOURCE: VILT GROUP, 2016.

VILT's model policy divided into energy efficiency, green purchasing and recycle, reuse and reduce gives a basis for how a company should commit itself after implementing Green IT. It is clear from this that responsibility does not end once an organisation has been certified.

The Exin institute provides the Green IT digital certification by providing training with online teaching material on all aspects of sustainable development and green IT. The main focus of the programme is to raise awareness among managers, which translates into more efficient use of energy and materials by IT professionals and IT users (EXIN[1], 2016).

The first certification is the Green IT Citizen, which provides the meaning of participating in a more sustainable way of working, reducing costs and contributing to the environment. This certification was developed for undergraduate IT students who work in technological environments (EXIN[2], 2016).

The Green IT Foundation certification is specific to IT professionals, business analysts, graduates, sustainability managers and business managers who are looking to improve business efficiency while reducing costs and their environmental impact (EXIN[3], 2016).

Alves (2016) warns about the need to obtain Green IT certifications due to the new roles of the IT manager:

> In addition, it is worth noting that with Green IT on the rise, two new IT roles are increasingly in demand: the IT Sustainability Analyst, who verifies, applies and configures the technical details of Green IT practices; and the IT Sustainability Manager, who defines and analyses plans and targets for the company to implement a system that makes IT sustainable, as well as presenting the return on investment (ROI) in adhering to Green IT.(2016, p.4)

Table 2 details the profile of these new IT professionals involved in Green IT:

Box 2: The roles of an IT professional specialising in Green IT

IT Sustainability Analyst - *(Green IT)*	IT Sustainability Manager - *(Green IT)*
Works with execution	Planning, control and coordination
Checks, applies and configures hardware and software for sustainable working mode.	Defines, creates and analyses the plans and targets needed to implement Green IT in the company.
Requires knowledge of hardware and software technologies	It requires skills in managing people, processes, products and partners.
Recommended certifications: EXIN Green IT Citizen. As well as technical certifications from hardware and	Recommended certifications: EXIN Green IT Citizen and EXIN Green IT Foundation. In addition to technical

software manufacturers (CCNA, MCSA/MCSE, LPI, etc.).	knowledge and certifications related to IT management (IT1L, COBIT, ISO-20000, ISO-27002, PMP/Prince2, etc.).
Academic level vision: Technical and/or Higher.	Academic level vision: Postgraduate MBA or specialisation.

SOURCE: ALVES, 2016, p.4

These new professional roles mean that managers need to be aware of how to coordinate Green IT through the certifications they already have, such as ITIL, COBIT and Prince2.

EPEAT certification makes it easier for companies to select high-performance electronic products that meet environmental criteria that address the product's complete life cycle, from energy conservation and toxic materials to product longevity and end-of-life management, serving the IT industry in a sustainable way. The system began in 2003 with a stakeholder process convened by the US Environmental Protection Agency and has grown

becoming the definitive global environmental rating system for electronic products (EPEAP, 2016).

Next, EPEAT[1] (2016) states that it currently includes product evaluations for PCs and Displays (including tablets), imaging equipment (which includes printers, copiers, scanners and multifunctional devices) and televisions and that environmental leadership standards are under development with the intention of forming the basis of future EPEAT categories for mobile phones, servers and other electronic products.

From a Green IT perspective, the benefits of this certification are shown in figure 7:

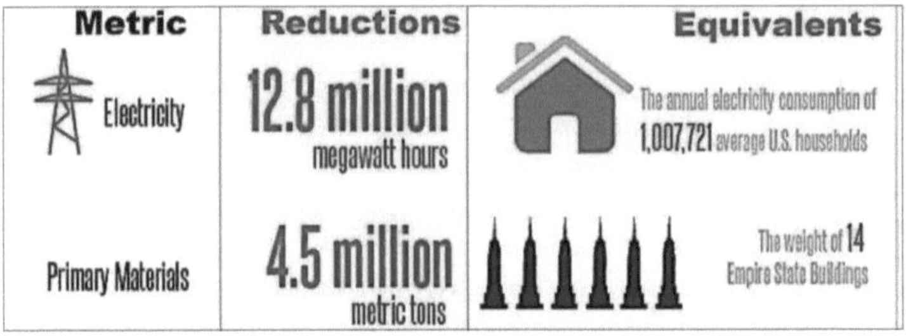

Figura 7: Environmental benefits

SOURCE: EPEAT[2], 2016.

Figure 7 presents the results of the EPEAT2 report (2016), showing that the benefits are truly measurable, i.e. there has been a saving of more than 12 million megawatts of electricity, enough to power 1,007,721 American homes for a year. The use of raw materials was reduced by 4.5 million tonnes, equivalent to the weight of 14 Empire State Buildings, and 0.6 tonnes of toxic materials were reduced, including mercury, enough to fill almost 1.1 million household mercury thermometers.

According to Reativa Energy Efficiency (2015), the Environmental Protection Agency created the Energy Star initially to certify computers and monitors and later to encourage manufacturers to create products with low energy consumption, reducing carbon dioxide emissions. The EPA applies the Energy Star label to commercial buildings , lighting, food service equipment, heating, cooling, ventilation, office equipment and household appliances.

In order to obtain this label, you need to follow certain requirements, which Reativa Energy Efficiency says all start with the Department of Energy's "Energy Guide" label, which is the famous yellow label that shops require on all large household appliances. This label displays the results of tests according to the Department of Energy's standard procedures.

The label lists how much energy the appliance consumes, compared to other similar products, and an estimate of the annual operating costs (the estimated annual operating costs are based on the average annual cost of electricity). If the product complies with the specific criteria for its category, which generally involve a percentage reduction in energy consumption compared to other products in the same category, the yellow label will be labelled Energy Star (Reactive Energy Efficiency, 2015).

The Procel Seal was created by the Federal Government and run by Eletrobrás, with the aim of being a simple and effective tool that allows consumers to find out which of the equipment and appliances available on the market are the most efficient and consume the least energy (PROCEL, 2006).

Consumption and performance indices are established for each category of equipment. Each piece of equipment that is a candidate for the Seal must undergo tests in laboratories which, according to Procel (2006), are indicated by Eletrobrás. Only products that meet these indices are awarded the Procel Seal.

The main areas of operation of the PROCEL label (2006) are the identification of the most efficient equipment and household appliances, the promotion of efficient energy use in the construction sector, in residential, commercial and public buildings, supporting town halls in the planning and implementation of projects to replace equipment and improve public lighting and traffic signs.

2.2.3 Metrics for Green IT

To calculate some of the benefits of Green IT in electronic products, there is the Electronics Environmental Benefits Calculator, which the

Environmental Protection Agency defines as follows:

> The EEBC estimates the environmental benefits of improving the acquisition, utilisation and disposal of computer products, specifically computer desktops, liquid crystal display (LCD) and cathode ray tube (CRT) monitors, notebooks and computers/laptops. The EEBC also calculates the benefits of mobile phone reuse and recycling, and of recycling mixed loads of electronic equipment. (EPA, 2012, p.1)

According to EPA (2012), table 3 shows the EPEAT criteria that are included in EEBC calculations based on products in the Silver standard:

Table 3: EEBC calculations

Criteria in BSE	EPEAT Reference	EPEAT's Si 1 see product profile
Hg. Gd, Grc +. PEB. PEDEj.	4.1.1.1 Hequendos	1 all products: bim
Hg ecl ara tion: number of lamps containing Hg: maximum Hg media content per lamp.	4.1.3.1 Hequendos	GPU: N I A.LULIs: 3 bulbs, 0.003 grams N otebo oks: 01 bulbs, 0 grams
Hg in the light; maximum average^mg Hg/bulb.	4.1.3.2 Optional	UPU: N/A LCD:yes N otebo oks: yes
Hg-free lamp.	4.1.3.3 Optional	CPU: 14/A LGD:none N otebo ok: yes
Recycled resin content of the product (10%; 25%).	4.2.1.2; 4.2.1.3 Optional	All products: No
Meets Energy Star® requirements.	4.5.1.1 Hequendos	1 all products: Eim
Recycled packaging content.	4.5.3.1 Required^ Statement Optional- the content%	UPU: 35% corrugated paper; 0% plastic; D% other. LGD: 50% corrugated cardboard: 5% plastic; 0% other. Notebook: 63% corrugated cardboard: 10% plastic; 4% other.
Minimum 2b% recycled content of corrugated cardboard packaging	4.5.3.2 Optional	All products: Yes
Reusable packaging	4.5.b 1 Optional	All products: none

SOURCE: EPA. 2012. p. 6 and 7. Adapted.

Table 3 uses the Energy Star label and the RoHS directive as a basis for establishing energy consumption levels, which are compared with products on the market without the label. The energy consumption data entered must be higher than the system's predefined rates, otherwise the benefits are not calculated (EPA, 2012, p.5).

The calculator works with a data entry form, where you can fill in all the data or insert an xml file formatted to the standards required by the EPA. Figure 8 shows the information equipment in use screen, with an emphasis on energy management and useful life, where data such as the quantity and Energy Star identification of desktop computers, CRT monitors, LED monitors and laptops must be entered.

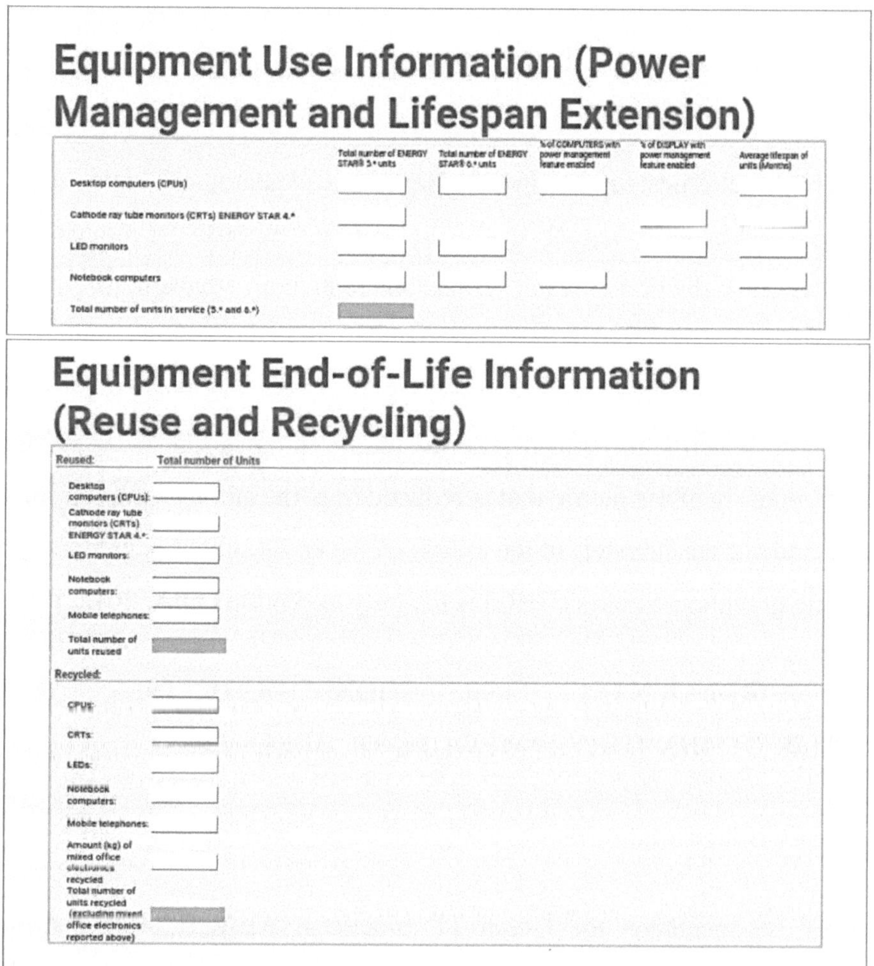

Figure 8: Print screen of the EEBC calculator

SOURCE: APP2

To run, the calculator depends on inputs such as the number of electronic products purchased, used, and/or disposed of, EPEAT registration, product lifespan (in months) and the weight of each product load (EPA, 2012, p.2). Because it is a modular system, the calculator can quantify the benefits of EPEAT-registered computer products, monitor energy management, increase the life-cycle of products, reuse desktops and recycle.

The Electronics Environmental Benefits Calculator calculates eight environmental benefits, namely energy savings, greenhouse gas reductions, air emission reductions, water emission reductions, hazardous waste reductions, toxic material reductions, primary material savings and cost reductions.

These benefits are considered "inventory" metrics that measure the mass or quantity of the metric that is reduced (e.g. the amount of hazardous waste), and not the "impact" of the metric on the environment (e.g. toxicity) Reducing greenhouse gases (GHG) is the only exception (EPA, 2012, p.9).

2.3 ENVIRONMENTAL LEGISLATION, GUIDELINES AND POLICIES WITHIN THE FRAMEWORK OF GREEN IT

2.3.1 REACH legislation

As an incentive for Green IT practices, REACH, Registration Evaluation and Authorisation of Chemicals, requires companies that use chemical substances, alone or in mixtures, in their industrial or professional activities, to transmit the information to the chemical producers or to the European Chemicals Agency (EUROPEAN UNION, 2006).

The registration of substances for manufacturers, importers and downstream users has conditions such as the substance being present in the articles in quantities that amount to more than one tonne per producer or importer per year, the substance being intended to be released under normal or reasonably foreseeable conditions of use and it must be present in the articles in a concentration of more than 0.1 % by mass (m/m).

The registration information must contain the identity and contact details of the producer or importer, registration numbers, the identity of the substance, the classification of the substance(s), a brief description of the use(s) of the substance contained in the article and the tonnage range of the substance(s).

This legislation has a direct impact on the chemical substances used in the production of computer components and their life cycle. Its aim is to guarantee a high level of protection for human health and the environment by promoting the development of alternative methods for assessing the dangers of substances, and to guarantee the free movement of substances within the internal market, while simultaneously strengthening competitiveness and innovation.

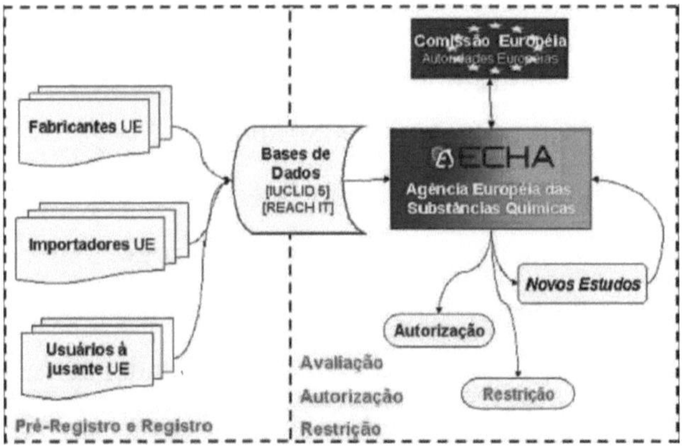

Figure 9: Overview of the processes involved in REACH

SOURCE: CRQ4, 2016.

All those included in the REACH legislation must draw up a chemical safety report for all registered substances, which must document the hazards to human health, physicochemical hazards and environmental hazards, including the assessment of persistent, bioaccumulative and toxic and very persistent and very bioaccumulative.

In Brazil, REACH is already having a major impact on importers, as companies such as Braskem and Petrobras are noticing a greater demand from customers for certification. Alpargatas had to replace the compounds called phthalates in the entire range of Havaianas flip-flops so that its products would not be prevented from entering European countries (ECODEBATE, 2013).

2.3.2RoHS Directive

One of the main objectives of Green IT is to minimise the incidence of toxic components, substances that are harmful to the environment and humans, such as mercury in LED screens and lead or lithium in laptop batteries. In Brazil there are regulations regarding electronic waste, but there are still no references to chemical exclusion in the production of components.

The RoHS directive, Restriction on the use of Hazardous Substances, in paragraphs 5, 6 and 7 (EUROPEAN PARLIAMENT, 2011) determines the elimination of substances with maximum concentration values by weight, tolerated in homogeneous materials of certain types of electrical and electronic equipment (EEE), sold in Europe as of 1 July 2006: lead (0.1%), mercury (0.1%), cadmium (0.01%), hexavalent chromium (0.1%), polybrominated biphenols (0.1%) (PBB), polybrominated diphenyl ethers (0.1%) (PBDE).

Figure 10 shows that the majority of companies were RoHS compliant before it was introduced in 2006.

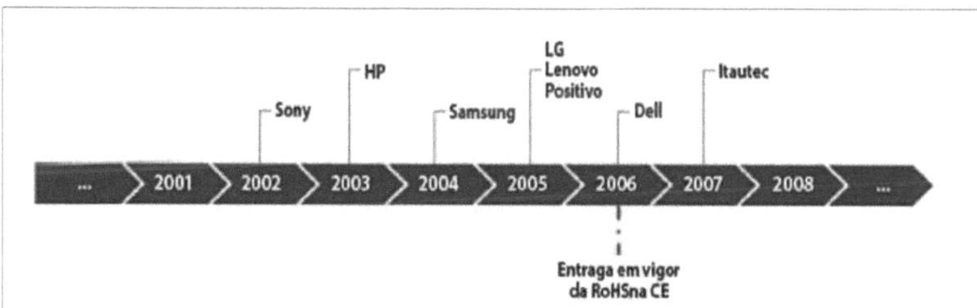

Figure 10: Chronology of companies' compliance with RoHS

SOURCE: BRESCANSIN (2015, p.42)

It is notable that many companies such as Sony, HP, Samsung, LG, Lenovo and Positivo were already prepared for these changes and took precautions. As a result, the directive makes companies concerned about recycling products that contain these substances, reducing the environmental impact and protecting the health of those who work with them.

Manufacturers must ensure that the EEE produced complies with the directive by developing all technical documentation of production procedures, including a declaration of conformity. These documents must be kept on file for up to 10 years after the dissemination of the product, and any

change in manufacturing must be documented. In the case of an imported product, it must go through all the assessment procedures and be documented.

The declaration of conformity must be drawn up exclusively by the company with the unique identification name of the product (so that it can be traced), the name and address of the manufacturer and be duly signed by the person responsible along with the date of issue.

According to Brescansin (2015, p.43), seven factors were identified that led to the adoption of Rohs, as shown in figure 11.

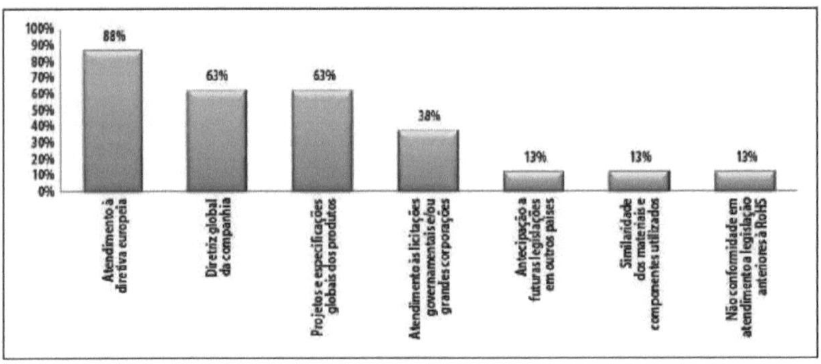

Figure 11: Factors motivating the adoption of RoHS by companies

SOURCE: BRESCANSIN (2015, p.43)

It can be seen that 88% of the companies were motivated to comply with the directive simply by the fact of "complying with the European directive", followed by "this being a global directive for the company" with 63%. The topic "because their projects and specifications are global" reached 63 per cent and for 38 per cent of the companies, "complying with government tenders and selling to large corporations" was the main motivator.

2.3.3 Cap and Trade environmental policy

In 1960, Ronald Coase, an economist at the University of Chicago, began promoting the idea of pollution trading, believing that pollution should be seen as part of the cost of production. If it was taxed as part of the production process, market forces would eventually stop companies polluting the environment (KILL, 2012, p.11).

In 1976, according to Kill (2012, p.11), the US Environmental Protection Agency (EPA) applied the concept of emissions trading to reduce the level of certain pollutants in the air. The US Clean Air Act was passed in 1990, a national sulphur dioxide trading system with the aim of combating the problem of acid rain.

Carbon trading is currently the centrepiece of international climate change policy. However, it is worth remembering that for Kill (2012, p.23) all existing cap and trade systems rely on measurement through a surrogate factor, using conversion factors between the different gases rather than direct measurement of the emission itself.

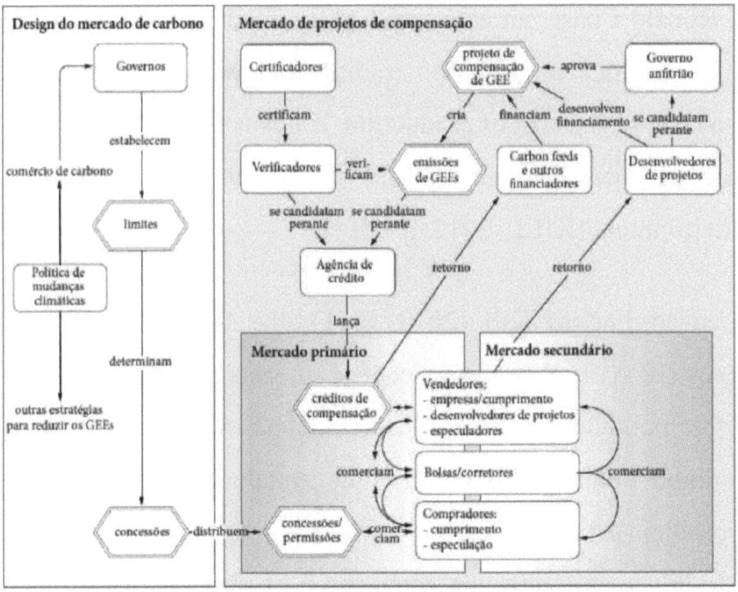

Figure 12: The carbon market in organisational chart form

SOURCE: KILL, 2012, p.97.

Figure 12 shows that permits or licences are units of pollution given to emitters within the framework of a cap and trade system. They are provided by a relevant authority, usually a government body . In the case of carbon permits, this is a licence to emit a certain amount of greenhouse gases (KILL, 2012, p.32).

In the offset project market, offset credits are the units that describe claimed emission reductions generated by projects

(KILL, 2012, p.32). In the regulated carbon market, credits are provided by the relevant authority, such as the CDM board of the Kyoto Protocol. In the voluntary market, credits are provided by the offset companies themselves. The European Commission (2016) works with the Cap and Trade principle, which is defined in terms of the total amount of certain greenhouse gases that can be emitted by factories, plants and other installations in the system, with the aim of reducing total emissions. Within the Green IT methodology, this principle discussed in figure 13 can contribute to the control and subsequent elimination of pollutant emissions.

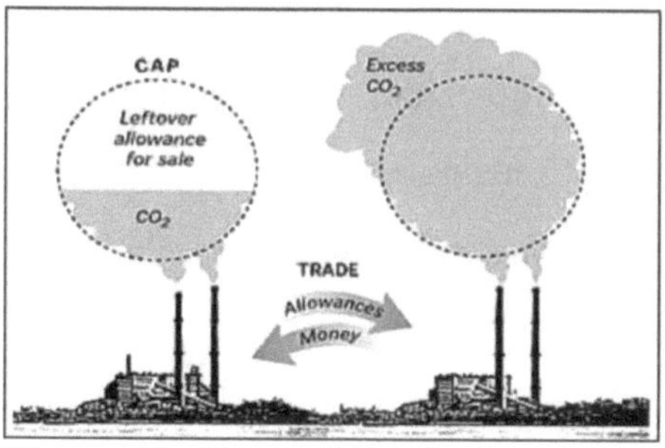

Figure 13: Cap and Trade System

SOURCE: FIRST CARBON SOLUTIONS, 2013.

The principle is necessary for some countries to reduce greenhouse gas emissions. Specifically, each country is allowed to release a certain amount of polluting gas into the air, which, when it isn't too much, can be sold in the form of a quota, known as a carbon credit. Some companies pollute so much that they exceed the emission limit and need to buy these credits from those that pollute the environment less.

The European Commission (2016) points out that companies receive or buy emission allowances that they can exchange with each other as needed. They can also buy limited quantities of international credits from emission reduction projects around the world. The limit on the total number of allowances available ensures that they have a value.

CHAPTER 3

FINAL CONSIDERATIONS

Given that IT has migrated from a focus on digitising data and information to the creation of applications and web access and, consequently, to business processes, it is still necessary for its applicability to consume an exorbitant amount of hardware, stressing that this consumption will not recede due to the fact that technology changes all the time, with new procedures, in other words, it ends up being volatile.

For an organisation, the replacement and disposal of hardware is necessary as it becomes obsolete or not compatible with current technology. On the other hand, we have consumerism on the part of society, which buys more electronic products without the need to get a new one.

We realise that the generation of e-waste is due to the facts discussed above, where computer equipment is consequently disposed of incorrectly. E-waste not only harms and contaminates the environment, but also the people who come into contact with it. As mentioned in subchapter 2.1.1, one of the biggest problems with e-waste and society is the lack of laws punishing manufacturers, the inspection of materials for recycling and the ineffectiveness of consumer information on how to dispose of electronic products.

The way in which the company relates to the environment has been discussed for a long time, and in this undergraduate work the entire history of Brazilian environmental policy has been covered, which has contributed to the organisation acquiring a vision of social and environmental responsibility, a vision acquired through its maturity in knowing that it must become aware of its role in society.

By becoming aware of its responsibility, the organisation sees environmental laws as extremely important and can implement the Green IT concept explained above. This makes it possible to balance environmental impacts, promoting environmentally sustainable development, one of the most important requirements for efficient and effective environmental management.

We mustn't forget that environmental concerns will always feature prominently in society, where they are influenced by politics, NGOs and environmental guidelines. The IT sector harms the environment through high electricity consumption, the disposal of hardware and the inefficient use of electronic equipment. By applying Green IT factors to the company, it becomes a necessary tool for controlling environmental damage.

Although this study deals with the conceptual side of Green IT, it is believed that obtaining certifications for the company, for managers and environmental seals can help the organisation adapt to the strict environmental standards that already exist. Remember that these standards are not only national, but also international.

It should be noted that environmental standards such as REACH and RoHS may soon become mandatory. As mentioned in the survey, some companies are already being influenced by them. Even though our country does not yet have policies specifically focused on the IT sector, organisations must adapt, as there is a need in the international market to preserve the environment.

Green IT turns out to be a tool for managing information technology that includes in its control factors not only the disposal of components, but also evaluates and applies corrections to all processes related to the area. As a result, organisations develop strategies for disposing of waste and electronic equipment, restructure the entire server layout and change the organisational culture.

The conclusion is that this study was intended to contribute to access to important information that contributes to Brazilian sustainability, encompassing both companies and society. As it was characterised as a study of theoretical foundations, it is recommended that other researchers look into this methodology in a practical way.

CHAPTER 4

REFERENCES

ALVES. Davis. **The Importance of Green IT Certifications for IT Professionals.** Exin, 2016. Available at: https://www.exin.com/BR/pt/exames/&fw=green-it. Accessed on: 12 July 2016.

APP2. **Electronics Environmental Benefits Calculator - Computer Products.** Available at: http://app2.erg.com/EEBC-Computerv4/eebcCalculator.do. Accessed on: 10 August 2016.

BRAZIL. **LAW NO. 12.305, OF 2 AUGUST 2010.** Establishes the National Solid Waste Policy; amends Law No. 9.605, of 12 February 1998; and makes other provisions. Available at: http://www.planalto.gov.br/ccivil_03/_ato2007-2010/20 10/lei/l12305.htm. Accessed on: 21 February 2016.

BOECHAT. Lucas. **E-waste management in Brazil.** 2015. Available at: https://techinbrazil.com.br/gerenciamento-de-lixo-eletronico-no-brasil. Accessed on: 15 October 2016.

BRAYNER, F. L. D. A.; RAMOS, P. G.; BRAYNER, P. V. D. A. **Green IT: Sustainability in information technology**. National Symposium on Health and the Environment. João Pessoa: SINAMASA. 2013.

BRESCANSIN. Ademir, et.al. **Restricting the use of hazardous substances (RoHS) in the personal computer segment: analysing the adoption strategy by manufacturers established in Brazil.** GEPROS. Gestão da Produção, Operações e Sistemas, Bauru, Year 10, No. 3, July-September 2015. Available at: http://revista.feb.unesp.br/index.php/gepros/article/viewFile/1281/670&ved. Accessed on: 25 October 2016.

CRQ4. **The implications of Reach for Brazil.** 2016. Available at:www.crq4.org.br/informativomat_147 . Accessed on: 22 October 2016.

ECODEBATE. **Reach: Legislation to control the entry of chemical products into the EU is already affecting Brazil.** 2013. Available at: https://www.ecodebate.com.br/2013/03/07/reach-legislacao-para-controle-da-entrada-de-produtos-quimicos- na-ue-ja-afeta-brasil/. Accessed on: 22

October 2016.

EPA. **Using the Electronics Environmental Benefits Calculator (EEBC).** Federal Electronics Challenge, 2012. Available at: https://www.epa.gov/sites/production/file s/documents/faq_eebc.pdf. Accessed on: 10 August 2016.

EPEAT[1]. **About EPEAT**. 2016. Available at: http://www.epeat.net/about-epeat/. Accessed on: 14 July 2016.

EPEAT[2]. **About EPEAT - Environmental benefits**. 2016. Available at: http://www. epeat.net/about-epeat/environmental-benefits/. Accessed on: 14 July 2016.

EUROPEAN COMMISSION. Climate Action. **The EU Emissions Trading System (EU ETS): A 'cap and trade' system**. 2016. Available at: <http://ec.europa.eu /clima/policies/ets/index_en.htm>. Accessed on: 27 March 2016.

EXIN[1]. **Exin Green IT**. 2016. Available at: https://www.exin.com/BR/pt/exames/&f w=green-it. Accessed on: 12 July 2016.

EXIN[2]. **Green IT Citizen**. 2016. Available at: https://www.exin.com/BR/pt/exame s/&exam=green-it-citizen?trk=profile_certification_title. Accessed on: 12 July 2016.

EXIN[3]. **Green IT Foundation**. 2016. Available at: https://www.exin.com/BR/pt/exa mes/&exam=exin-green-it-foundation. Accessed on: 12 July 2016.

FAVERA. Eduardo Ceretta Dalla. **Electronic Waste and Society**. Federal University of Santa Maria, 2008. Available at: http://www-usr.inf.ufsm.br/~faver a/elc1020/t1/artigo-elc1020.pdf. Accessed on: 15 October 2016.

FERNANDES, A.A. & KUGLER, J.L.C.: **Systems Project Management: A Practical Approach**. 2nd Edition. LTC - Livros Técnicos e Científicos Ed., 1990.

FILLETI. Rômulo Augusto Padovezi, et.al. **Green IT 2005-2015: A systematic literature review**. 5th Brazilian Congress of Production Engineering. Ponto

Grossa, PR, Brazil, 02 to 04 December 2015. Available at:www.aprepro.org.br/conbrepro/2015/down.php?id=1188&q=1 . Accessed on: 22 February 2016.

FIRST CARBON SOLUTIONS. **Carbon Emissions Cap and Trade in California is Here to Stay**. 2013. Available at: info.firstcarbonsolutions.com/blog/bid/266085/Ca rbon-Emissions-Cap-and-Trade-in-California-is-Here-to-Stay. Accessed on: 29 July 2016.

FRESCHI. Prof Me. Julio Cesar, et.al. **The evolution of IT and its impact on business administration**. Revista Terceiro Setor, v.7, n°1, 2013. Available at: revistas.ung.br/index.php/3setor/article/view/1907/1502. Accessed on: 17 October 2016.

GUPTA, S. **Computing with Green responsibility**. Proceedings of the International Conference and Workshop on Emerging Trends in Technology, 2010.

JUNIOR. Eloy Fassi Casagrande. **Technological innovation and sustainability: Possible tools for a necessary interface**. Federal Technological Education Centre of Paraná, 2004. Available at: http://ucbweb.castelobranco.br/webcaf/arquivos/28782/9292/InovacaoTecnologica_e_Sustentabilidade2004. pdf. Accessed on: 15 May 2016.

KILL. Jutta et.al. **Carbon trading: how it works and why it's controversial**. Translated by Leandro Moura and Priscila Moura. Rio de Janeiro: Heinrich Boll Foundation; United Kingdom: FERN, 2012.

LADEIRA. Wagner Junior, et.al. **Green IT and the Information Production Process: An Analysis of Activities that Produce Environmental Sustainability.** XXXIII ANPAD Meeting. São Paulo / SP - 19 to 23 September 2009. Available at: http://www.anpad.org.br/diversos/trabalhos/EnANPAD/enanpad_2009/ADI/2009_ADI1675.pdf. Accessed on: 22 February 2016.

LAURINDO. Fernando José Barbin et.al. **The role of information technology (IT) in the strategy of organisations**. Gestão & Produção v.8, n.2, p.160-179, aug. 2001. Available at: http://www.scielo.br/pdf/gp/v8n2/v8n2a04. Accessed on: 15 May 2016.

LUNARDI. Guilherme Lerch, et.al. **Green IT: an analysis of the main benefits and practices used by organisations.** Scielo, 2012. Available at:

http://www.scielo.br/scielo.php?pid=S1413-23112014000100001&script=sci_arttext. Accessed on: 23 February 2016.

MAGGIOLINI, P.: **Costs and Benefits of an Information System**. Italy, ETAS LIBRI, 1981.

MARRONI. Róger. **Study guide for the Green IT Citizen certification**. Cesta de Conhecimentos, 2014. Available at: http://cestadeconhecimentos.com.br/cc /ebook-green-it-citizen-the-study-guide-for-the-certification/. Accessed on: 22 February 2016.

MANZINI. E; Vezzoli. C. **The development of sustainable products - the environmental requirements of industrial products**. São Paulo> EDUSP, 368p. 2002.

MINGAY. SIMON. **Green IT: The New Industry Shock Wave.** Gartner, 7 December 2007. Available at: download.microsoft.com/.../VirtualisationPublicSafe. Accessed on: 21 February 2016.

MORAES. Samuel de Barros, et.al. **Adoption of Green IT practices in a company. Case study of a Call Centre company**. X Postgraduate and Research Workshop of the Paula Souza Centre. São Paulo, 6 - 8 October 2015 ISSN: 2175-1897. Available at: http://www.centropaulasouza.sp.gov.br/pos-graduacao/workshop-de-pos-graduacao-e-pesquisa/010-workshop-2015/workshop/tr abalhos/Sistemas_Produtivos/Gest_Estrat_TI/Adocao_de_praticas_Green_IT.pdf.
Accessed on: 22 February 2016.

EUROPEAN PARLIAMENT. **Directive 2011/65/EU of the European Parliament and of the Council of 8 June 2011** on the restriction of the use of certain hazardous substances in electrical and electronic equipment (recast) (Text with EEA relevance). p. 1-37, 2011. Available at: <http://eur-lex.europa.eu/legal-content/PT/TXT/?uri=CELEX:32011L0065>.
Accessed on: 27 March 2016.

PROCEL. **The programme**. 2006. Available at: http://www.procelinfo.com.br/main.as p?TeamID=%7B88A19AD9-04C6-43FC-BA2E-99B27EF54632%7D. Accessed on: 15 July 2016.

REACTIVE ENERGY EFFICIENCY. **How Energy Star works**. 2015. Available at: http://reativaeficienciaenergetica.blogspot.com.br/2015/04/como-funciona-o-energy-star.html?m=1. Accessed on: 15 July 2016.

SACILOTTI. Adaní Cusin. **The importance of Information Technology in micro and small companies: an exploratory study in the Jundiaí region**. Campo Limpo Paulista College, 2011. Available at: http://www.faccamp.br/site/arq/pdf/m estrado/Documentos/producao_discente/2011/04abril/AdaniCusinSacilotti/dissertaC Ao.pdf. Accessed on> 15 October 2016.

SILVA. Danielly Ferreira, et.al. **Companies and the environment: contributions from environmental legislation**. INTERthesis International Interdisciplinary Journal, vol.10, n°2, 2013. Available at: https://periodicos.ufsc.br/index.php/interthesis/article/vie w/1807-1384.2013v10n2p334/25926. Accessed on: 15 October 2016.

TACHIZAWA. Takeshy. **Environmental management and corporate social responsibility: business strategies focussed on the Brazilian reality**. 6 ed. revised and expanded. São Paulo: Atlas, 2010.

EUROPEAN UNION. **Regulation (EC) No 1907/2006 of the European Parliament and of the Council:** concerning the Registration, Evaluation, Authorisation and Restriction of Chemicals (REACH), establishing a European Chemicals Agency, amending Directive 1999/45/EC and repealing Council Regulation (EEC) No 793/93 and Commission Regulation (EC) No 1488/94 as well as Council Directive 76/769/EEC and Directives 91/155/EEC, 93/67/EEC, 93/68/EEC, 93/68/EEC, and repealing **Regulation (EC) No 1907/2006**Council Regulation (EEC) No 793/93 and Commission Regulation (EC) No 1488/94 as well as Council Directive 76/769/EEC and Commission Directives 91/155/EEC, 93/67/EEC, 93/105/EC and 2000/21/EC (Text with EEA relevance). p. 1-278, 2006. Available at: <http://eur-lex.europa.eu/LexUriServ/LexUriServ.do?uri=OJ:L:2007:136:0003:0280:P T:PDF>. Accessed on: 27 March 2016.

VILT GROUP. **VILT is Green IT certified**. 2016. Available at: https://www.vilt-group.com/pt/sobre-vilt/certificacao-green-it. Accessed on: 18 October 2016.

MIX
Papier aus verantwortungsvollen Quellen
Paper from responsible sources
FSC® C105338

Printed by Books on Demand GmbH, Norderstedt / Germany